Santi & Naz

Created by Guleraana Mir and Madelaine Moore

**Written by Guleraana Mir and
afshan d'souza-lodhi**

methuen | drama

LONDON • NEW YORK • OXFORD • NEW DELHI • SYDNEY

METHUEN DRAMA
Bloomsbury Publishing Plc, 50 Bedford Square, London, WC1B 3DP, UK
Bloomsbury Publishing Inc, 1385 Broadway, New York, NY 10018, USA
Bloomsbury Publishing Ireland, 29 Earlsfort Terrace,
Dublin 2, D02 AY28, Ireland

BLOOMSBURY, METHUEN DRAMA and the Methuen
Drama logo are trademarks of Bloomsbury Publishing Plc.

First published in Great Britain 2025

Cover design by Becca White

Cover photography by Greg Veit

Bloomsbury Publishing Plc does not have any control over, or responsibility
for, any third-party websites referred to or in this book. All internet addresses
given in this book were correct at the time of going to press. The author and
publisher regret any inconvenience caused if addresses have changed or sites
have ceased to exist, but can accept no responsibility for any such changes.

A catalogue record for this book is available from the British Library.

A catalog record for this book is available from the Library of Congress.

ISBN: PB: 978-1-3505-6201-1
ePDF: 978-1-3505-6202-8
eBook: 978-1-3505-6203-5

Series: Modern Plays

Typeset by Mark Heslington Ltd, Scarborough, North Yorkshire

For product safety related questions contact
productsafety@bloomsbury.com

To find out more about our authors and books visit
www.bloomsbury.com and sign up for our newsletters.

Santi & Naz

Created by Guleraana Mir and Madelaine Moore
Written by Guleraana Mir and afshan d'souza-lodhi
Directed by Madelaine Moore

Santi & Naz was first produced by The Thelmas at VAULT
Festival 2020 where it won an Origins Award for
Outstanding New Work. After further development the play
was awarded the Charlie Hartill Fund and ran at Pleasance
Courtyard, Edinburgh Festival Fringe 2023. In 2024 *Santi &
Naz* embarked on a national tour supported by Arts Council
England. The tour culminated in a 3-week run at Soho
Theatre in January 2025, produced by The Thelmas and
Pleasance.

2024 Tour Dates

8–10 October Wardrobe Theatre, Bristol

11–13 October Beck Theatre, Hayes

16–17 October Tron, Glasgow

19 October Nottingham Playhouse

22 October The Place, Bedford

25–26 October Hippodrome, Birmingham

29 October Norwich Theatre

31 October Norern Stage, Newcastle

2 November Octagon Theatre, Bolton

7 November Attenborough Arts Centre, Leicester

8 November Derby Theatre

The 2025 production at Soho Theatre is produced by
The Thelmas and Pleasance, supported by
Arts Council England.

About The Thelmas

The Thelmas is an award-winning female-led theatre company established to develop and promote female-led artistic work that gives space to marginalised voices. We do this by telling playfully disruptive stories that appeal to diverse audiences and bridge the gap between the political and the mainstream. Our work is thought-provoking, complex and boisterous. Through our public productions, community-building and women-centred workshops, we explore the social, political and cultural stories that matter in fresh and surprising ways.

Our productions include *Coconut* by Guleraana Mir (Ovalhouse and national tour 2018); *Ladykiller* by Madeline Gould (Pleasance 2018, VAULT 2019, national tour and Brits Off Broadway selection 2020); *Notch* by Danaja Wass (VAULT 2020); *Santi & Naz* (VAULT 2020, Pleasance 2023, national tour 2024 and Soho Theatre 2025) and Fringe First winner *Son Of A Bitch* by Anna Morris (Summerhall 2024 and Southwark Playhouse 2025).

The company is led by director, Madelaine Moore and writer, Guleraana Mir.

www.thethelmas.co.uk

About Madelaine Moore, Artistic Director of The Thelmas

Madelaine Moore is an award-winning stage and screen director. Twice shortlisted for the Sir Peter Hall Director's Award and an Old Vic 12 Director, her work is informed by her interest in disrupting traditional gendered narratives and tackling big ideas through a feminist lens in surprising and irreverent ways, through playfulness with form or subverting common tropes.

Madelaine's debut short film as writer/director, *Twitching* was selected for multiple international film festivals (including

BAFTA and BIFA qualifying festivals). It was nominated for Best Screenplay at Little Venice Film Festival and won the Audience Award for Best UK Film at Poppy Jasper International Film Festival in 2023.

Theatre credits include: *The Ice at the End of the World* (Omnibus); *Son of a Bitch* (Summerhall, Southwark Playhouse); *Outpatient* (Summerhall, Reading Rep and The Lowry); *Glacier* (Old Fire Station); *Edith* (Lowry and Theatr Clwyd); *Gobble Gobble Gobble Gobble Goblin* (Old Vic Theatre); *Ladykiller* (national tour, Brits Off Broadway); *Evelyn* (Mercury Theatre, Southwark Playhouse); *Second Person Narrative* (Arcola Theatre); *The Awakening* (Jack Studio); *Algorithms* (Soho Theatre, Park Theatre, Netflix Stage to Screen winner); *Santi & Naz* (Soho Theatre and national tour, Charlie Hartill winner).

About Guleraana Mir, Executive Director of The Thelmas

Guleraana Mir is an award-winning writer and theatre maker. She is passionate about telling authentic stories that celebrate not stereotype, and speak to complex social realities in a fresh and disruptive way. She specialises in developing new work through devising and writing with young people and community groups, and leads writing programmes for artists of all ages at a number of institutions.

Guleraana has had writer's residencies at Soho Theatre and Shakespeare's Globe. She was a recipient of the Genesis Kickstart Fund in 2021 for her play *I Am The Ghost of Qandeel Baloch*, a member of the BBC Writersroom North cohort of 2018/19 and Junior Writer on Sky Studio's *The Rising* in 2020. She currently has an original TV series in development with afshan d'souza-lodhi.

Her credits include: *Santi & Naz* (co-writer, Soho Theatre and national tour); *At What Cost?*, *Take a Chance On Me*, *The Testing Place* for BBC's *Doctors* (Series 24); *Here we are* (Old

Vic Primary Play project); *here, here, here* (Stratford East Young Company); *All the Small Things* (BBC Children's); *Misfits* (co-writer, Queen's Theatre Hornchurch); *The Bigger Picture* (audio, commissioned by Tamasha and SOAS); *We're Just Getting Started* (Royal Exchange Theatre Young Company) and *Coconut* (Ovalhouse and national tour).

About afshan d'souza-lodhi

afshan d'souza-lodhi was born in Dubai and forged in Manchester. She is a writer of scripts and poetry. Her work has been performed and translated into numerous languages across the world. afshan has been writer-in-residence for Sky Studios, New Writing North, Royal Exchange Theatre, Warner Bros. Discovery and was writer-in-residence for Bluebird Pictures. afshan was also one of the first to receive the National Theatre's Peter Shaffer award in 2022.

afshan has been a BAFTA BFI Flare mentee and has developed a TV series with Sky Studios. A TV pilot she wrote called *Chop Chop*, was selected for the second annual #MuslimList (The Black List).

As well as her own writing, afshan is keen to develop other younger and emerging artists and sits on the boards of Manchester Literature Festival, Pie Radio and Royal Exchange Theatre Manchester. She is also the WGGB regional chair of Manchester and Lancashire.

www.afshandl.com

Cast

National tour 2024 and Soho Theatre 2025

Santi – Aiyana Barlett

Naz – Farah Ashraf

The production at Pleasance Courtyard in 2023 featured

Santi – Rosie-Marie Christian

Naz – Karendip Phull

Creative Team

National tour 2024 and Soho Theatre 2025

Movement Director – Rakhee Sharma

Associate Director – Vikesh Godhwani

Set and Costume Design – Sascha Gilmour

Associate Costume Designer – Kritika Agarwal

Lighting Designer – Laura Howard

Sound Design and Composition – Tom Penn

Technical Stage Manager – Brent Tan

General Manager – Courtenay Johnson

Setting and Staging

The play is set in different locations in the village where Santi and Naz live and the 'dreamscape' – a liminal space where they share their dreams, nightmares and premonitions.

The village is located in rural Punjab in India. It would have traditionally included a number of places of worship, communal cooking facilities, an area reserved for the men to meet. It could be based on present day Phatta, near to the India/Pakistan border.

The play begins in 1949 with Santi writing her book, and jumps backwards to 1945 where we follow the girls through their lives up to the moment of Partition in August 1947. Occasionally we return to 1949 with Santi narrating a memory, which then begins to play out in real time.

The characters are aged 13–17 over the course of the play. They are young, naive and have lived very sheltered lives; their innocence should be palpable. The play charts their journey to the understanding that young women have no control over their lives.

As with most global events, it is the social and personal stories that go unheard, especially the experiences of women. This play presents a historical moment through a modern lens, with Santi and Naz feeling like two ordinary girls audiences can relate to as easily as they might relate to a pair of teenagers at a bus stop in suburban London. It allows the audience to understand the political and historical context of the girls' lives by centring their experiences; giving voice to those who lived through Partition.

The Thelmas' production of *Santi & Naz* utilises minimal set and props. Sascha Gilmour's design consists of two pieces of wall sitting on opposite ends of a beautifully painted lino floor. From one of the walls a piece of fabric emerges to represent the girls' lake. Towards the end of the play Naz uses her dupatta to represent Nadeem. Aside from their books and jewellery we don't believe anything else is necessary, and encourage any future productions to make the most of actors' natural ability to create magic on stage.

Some Thoughts on History as a Lived Experience

Dr Eleanor Newbigin

How we understand the end of British rule in the Indian subcontinent has changed dramatically since it took place in August 1947. Initially, these developments were seen as a cause for celebration, both by the governments of the newly independent states of India and Pakistan, and by the former colonies who celebrated what they saw as a peaceful handover of power. With its focus on the legitimacy of state power, all of these accounts sidelined the brutal violence and mass migration that was reshaping the subcontinent in this period. This was 'partition', an unfortunate side effect of the main event: independence.

In the decades that has followed, this division has been called into question. Historians, social activists and citizens alike have helped to show that, while politicians may have seen 1947 as independence, for the millions of people killed and forced to migrate, partition was not a side effect of 1947 but the main event. This has produced not just different accounts of 1947 but different understandings of what constitutes history and where to look for it. Traditional history writing has tended to prioritise grand narratives at the expense of lived experience.

While it's important to piece together what happened in August 1947, the question of what people *thought* was happening and how they felt also brings insight into understanding how people acted as they did. Rather than being the 'small stories' of history, personal experiences are the stuff of which 'big historical narratives' are made. The question is though, how to uncover these experiences?

While the state leaves copious archives, what are the sources we can use if we want to write histories beyond the state, that see events from the perspective of ordinary people? Oral history has provided rich new sources for understanding partition but so too has fiction. History writing looks back on the past from the present. Fiction can help us to see another way, by helping us to put ourselves in the shoes of those who experienced it.

Santi & Naz may not be 'real' history but it plays an important role in helping us all engage with and see the events of 1947 from a different perspective: not as something that happened over 70 years ago to other people in a distant land, but as something that impacted human beings who were as real, complicated and full of feeling as ourselves.

Dr. Eleanor Newbigin is Senior Lecturer in the History of Modern South Asia at SOAS, University of London.

About Soho Theatre

Soho Theatre is London's most vibrant producer for new theatre, comedy and cabaret. A charity and social enterprise, we are driven by a passion for the work we produce, the artists we work with and the audiences we attract.

Our roots date back to the early 1970s at the Soho Poly Theatre. Small but influential, Soho Poly was radical and relevant, capturing the excitement and innovation of its time. Today our work is wide-ranging, drawing from this fringe heritage, and adding a queer, punk, counter-culture flavour. We champion voices that challenge from outside the mainstream, and sometimes from within it too. We value entertainment and a great night out.

We produce and co-produce new plays, work with associate artists and present the best new emerging theatre companies and comedians. We present the early work of countless UK artists (many who become industry giants), and we present many international artists' London debuts. We have a thriving variety of artist and talent development programmes, artists under commission and in development, and two new writing awards including the Verity Bargate Award for new playwrights.

Work extends far beyond our Dean Street home, with a UK and international touring programme and connections. We present shows and scout talent at Edinburgh Festival Fringe and are the UK's leading presenter of Indian comedians and regularly present work there. We film shows and create our own digital work that can be seen across our social platforms and inflight. And we are working towards opening our second London venue, Soho Theatre Walthamstow.

sohotheatre.com I @sohotheatre I @sohotheatreindia

Santi & Naz

Notes on Script

. . . Indicates an unspoken reaction

/   Indicates an overlap in dialogue

–   Indicates an interruption

Translation for any words in Urdu/Hindi/Punjabi are given in bold

1949

A soundscape of **Nehru**'s *speech of independence sets the scene.*

Nehru   Long years ago, we made a tryst with destiny, and now the time comes when we shall redeem our pledge, not wholly or in full measure, but very substantially. At the stroke of the midnight hour, when the world sleeps, India will awake to life and freedom.

Santi *and* **Naz** *find each other in the dreamspace, they play before returning to 1949.* **Santi** *writes in her book.*

Santi   The city is nothing like we imagined Naz. From what I can see from my window it is busy and no one stops to smell the chambeli **(jasmine)**. Even when the barefoot street children try and push it through the rolled-down windows of town cars.

When the horns beeping at night keep me awake. I stare at the cracks in the wall that look like slug trails and remind myself how much worse it could be. Baba says I am lucky. I tell him it is because I spent all that time dancing in the rain with you.

Do you remember how it felt to jump into our lake after a long day at school? How you would tease me when I wanted to finish my reading before joining you! I read even more now. I write the things I would rather forget and I think of you often, but you know that, don't you?

I think of you at the foot of our tree, with your feet in the water as the rain splashes down. You watch the ripples from each raindrop spread further and further, and smile.

It begins to rain.

Barsaat, 1945

Santi   Barsaat. **(Monsoon)**.

The first rain of the monsoon season is always the strongest. Or maybe that's just how it feels when the droplets hit your skin. I lift my face to the sky and let it wash over me, wash away the dust of the day.

Naz   Ajo nah! **(Come on!)**

Santi   There were so many errands to run. Your baba wasn't as strict as mine. (*Beat.*) Chalo nah. **(Let's go)**.

Naz   Santi!

Santi   Don't you care about what happens to me?

Naz   Don't be such a buddhi **(old woman)**.

Santi   Do you care about anything?

Naz   Barsaat brings good luck you know. Do you feel it?

Santi   I feel it.

Naz   I feel it on my arms.

Santi   I feel it in my hair.

Naz   I feel it in my belly.

Santi   I feel it as my feet splash the puddles.

Naz (*splashing her feet too*)   I feel it too!

Santi   I feel it in my ruha **(soul)**.

Naz   In your soul? Wah! What a writer, ji!

Santi   Me?

Naz   I'm telling you. One day you'll live in the city –

Santi   I'm never leaving this village.

Naz   And be *so* famous I'll have to make an appointment to come visit. Hey Santi, will you write about us? Write a bestseller.

Santi   I'll probably end up growing sugar cane –

Naz   And I'll say to my husband, 'Oh you know, my old saheli **(friend)** Santi . . .'

Santi   Husband? Wah! Now who's dreaming!

Naz   I could have a husband.

Naz *sticks her tongue out at* **Santi**.

Santi   Yeah, right!

They both stare at each other for a moment and then burst into laughter.

Both   Eewwwwww. Husband.

Naz *sticks her tongue out again. As she does, she catches the rain. It tastes good.*

Naz   Mmmm. Yummy!

Santi *also sticks out her tongue and catches the rain.*

Santi   Sweeter than shakarkandi **(sweet potato)**.

They both play in the rain enjoying each raindrop as it falls. Laughter.

Who Dat?

The girls are play-fighting – kushti.

Santi (*counting in Punjabi*)   One, two –

Before she can get to three **Naz** *launches herself at* **Santi**.

Santi   Every time you cheat.

Naz   I thought you said *on* three.

Santi   It's after three, and you know it.

Naz   Yaar **(dude)**, I forgot nah.

Santi   Whatever.

Naz   Chalo. Start again. I'll count this time.

Santi   We go *after* three, OK?

Naz   Yup. One, two –

As **Naz** *lunges for* **Santi**, *she jumps out of the way, anticipating that* **Naz** *is going to cheat again.*

Santi   You promised!

Naz   You should know better than to trust me –

Santi   Kushti time.

Santi *lunges at* **Naz**. *They wrestle.*

Naz   Have you been practicing?

Santi   Maybe.

Naz   With who?

Santi   Not telling.

Naz   But you tell me everything.

Santi   Do I?

Naz   Don't you?

Santi   I save my secrets for my bestest best friend.

Naz   Errr . . . and who's that?

Santi   Wouldn't you like to know.

Naz   Yes. I would actually.

Santi   Well lucky for you, I am about to tell you . . .

Naz   Don't you dare say the goat.

Santi   It's . . .

Santi *is distracted.*

Naz   Yes? Santi? You're meant to say me. (*Beat.*) It's always me. You always say it's me.

Santi *is staring at something, or someone.*

Santi   Who is that?

Naz   Who?

Santi   Do you know him?

Naz   Who you talking about?

Santi *grabs* **Naz** *and shows her.*

Both   Oooooooh.

Santi   What do you think he's doing here?

Naz   Dunno.

Santi   His arms are so smooth and curvy. His hair is so shiny. I like that it's curly.

Naz   Mine's curly too –

Santi   Who thought men's hair would look so good so curly?

Naz   Sort of. Not really but –

Santi   What's he handing out? Oh my god, did he write those? Is he a writer? Naz! I think he's a writer!

Naz (*with sarcasm*)   Match made in heaven.

Santi   I can't tell what he's saying. Can you? Can you look? Please, Naz.

Naz *peers forward to get a better look, she reads their lips.*

Naz   Boring stuff.

Santi   Tell me.

Naz   He is saying, 'Here take this. You need to take my book. Take it!'

Santi   Are you sure? It's not a book, it's a paper.

Naz   Yeah, that's what I meant. Paper. Paper and book look the same on your lips, nah.

Santi *repeats book and paper multiple times trying to figure out if they look the same on your lips.*

Santi   You can't lip read! Are you making this all up?

Naz   Can too – Abba taught me.

Santi   I don't believe you.

Naz   Why don't you ask your bestest best friend?

Santi   That's you silly. It's always you. I was just building up the tension.

Naz   I knew that. He *is* saying something important.

Santi   How do you know?

Naz   Look how he's waving his arms around.

Santi   Oh yeah.

Naz *waves her arms around as if gesticulating passionately.* **Santi** *joins her. It becomes a bit of a dance.*

Teeyan, 1945

The girls fool about dancing for teeyan. **(Teeyan is a festival celebrated throughout Punjab which is dedicated to the onset of the monsoon. It focuses on daughters, sisters and mothers. In the past, married women would return to their maternal house to participate in the festivities.)** *They imitate various people from the village and end up with Gandhi and Jinnah.*

Santi Um hello. I am Mister Gandhi and I have silly glasses and I talk about Indians like I know everything about all of them. *All of them.*

(To **Naz**.*)* Including you. But I don't.

(Aside, as herself.) He doesn't know about us, about our gaon **(village)**.

Naz Yeah, he doesn't know about us, or our village. My go! *(She becomes Gandhi.)*

Do or die! We shall either free India or die in the attempt; we shall not live to the per, perp, perpeetto –

Santi *(as herself)* Perpetuation?

Naz That. Of our slavery –

Santi *(as herself)* Continue . . .

Naz Every true man or woman or child or donkey or goat or murghi **(chicken)** or –

Santi *(as herself)* Er, Naz?

Naz *(as herself)* The rest of it has really big words nah. You do it.

Santi Say it with me. Every true Congressman or woman.

Both Every true Congressman or woman.

Santi Will join the struggle with inflexible determination.

Naz Will join the struggle with in-flex-ible determination.

Santi   Not to remain alive to see the country in bondage and slavery.

Naz   Not to remain alive to see the country.

Santi   In bondage and slavery.

Naz   In bondage and slavery. (*Beat.*) What does that even mean?

Santi   I dunno. My go!

Naz   Please, Jinnah Saheb, take the microphone.

She mock bows. **Santi** *bows back and takes on the physicality of Jinnah.*

Santi   Thank you, Gandhiji. Now that you have finished I shall speak because I think that I am *also* big and important and mean and blah blah blah blah –

Naz   Jinnah Sahib?

Santi (*as Jinnah*)   I am not taking questions right now. I am telling you eighty millions of Musalmans in India have nothing to fear. They have their destiny in their hands, and –

Naz (*as herself*)   I know this! There is magic in our hands.

Santi (*as Jinnah*)   NO! There is magic power in *your own* hands. Think a hundred times –

Naz (*as herself*)   How do I think a hundred times?

Santi (*as Jinnah*)   Just think before you take any decision, but once it is taken, stand by it as one man or woman.

Naz   OK OK. Now I have a serious thought.

Santi (*as Jinnah*)   You must wait your turn, I am still speaking. No one likes little girls that think.

Naz   But, have you met Mr Gandhi's goat?

Santi (*as Jinnah*)   Oh little girl, your country is on the brink of change and all you care about is some stupid animal.

The girls go back to being themselves.

Naz   Goats are clever, you know.

Santi   Your goat ate my chappal **(sandals)**.

Naz   My Abba bought you a new pair, didn't he?

Santi   Yeah.

Santi *begins to reorganise the space for Teeyan.*

Naz   What does revolution mean?

Santi   Why?

Naz   Abba says that we should prepare for revolution.

Santi   Why was he talking about revolution?

Naz   I don't even know what it means.

Santi   It means we can finally kick the last of the Angrez **(English)** out.

Naz   What will happen when the British leave?

Santi   Why, you want to marry one?

Naz   Noo! I want one of their biiiig houses. Do you think Muslims will be allowed to live in them?

Santi   It doesn't matter if you're Muslim or I'm Sikh or our friends are Hindu, we're all the same inside. We'll all get big, beautiful bungalas **(mansions)** of our own. But only when –

Naz   But Abba says –

Santi   Don't you feel how alive the village gets when Holi or Eid comes around? You'll come to my big mansion for Diwali. And We'll all do Teeyan together in the gardens. Now let's go eat. I smell pooris!

Naz   Thought you didn't like Teeyan.

Santi   Never said that. Besides, I'm never leaving this village . . . so I'll never have to celebrate coming back!

Naz   Not even when you get married?

Santi   Not even when I get married.

Naz   I'm never getting married.

Santi   Never?

Naz   Never, ever. Kabhee bhee nahin (**never**).

Santi   Then me neither.

They hold hands and spin, singing, clapping, dancing. The dancing segues into the next scene as the lake is made.

Books at the Lake

At the lake. **Santi** *is encouraging* **Naz** *to read a book in English.*

Naz   What's the point of learning English, if they're leaving?

Santi   You love English.

Naz   *You* love English.

Santi   And you love me, so read.

Naz   But it's so boring. And plain, and –

Santi   And you have to learn it.

Naz   But whyyyyyyy?

Santi   Everyone uses English in the offices –

Naz   Imagine *me* in an office. I'd finally meet an Angrez **(white person)** up close and I'd type all his important notes. On one of those typewriters.

Santi   Oooh, a Remington. Yes please.

Naz (*she pretends to type with two fingers*)   Look Santi! I'm you.

Santi   What are you typing?

Naz   A story.

Santi   About?

Naz   Dau larkiyan. Ek jo hai bohth, parhi likhi – **(Two girls. One who is very educated –)**

Santi   In English.

Naz   Santi!

Santi   Practice makes perfect.

Naz   Ooof. Meri dost ho, o kya? **(Are you my friend or what?)**

Santi   I am your bestest best friend.

Naz   So?

Santi   Acha, theek hai **(OK, fine)**. I'll tell the story, you translate.

Naz   Teamwork!

Santi   Ek din, India meh – **(One day in India –)**

Naz   Slowly!

Santi   . . .

Naz   Say it again then.

Santi (*exaggerated slowly*)   Ek din, India meh –

Naz (*slowly*)   One day in India.

Santi   Ek shehr. **(A lion.)**

Naz   Rahul!

Santi   I mean, we could call him Rahul, but there are better names for Lions.

Naz   But this Rahul has nice arms . . .

Santi   Kya? **(What?)**

Naz   Your guy, the one with the arms.

Santi   He's not *my* guy.

Naz   I followed him. To the nimboo paani stand.

Santi   You did what?

Naz   I pretended I wanted some lemonade and I heard the nimboo paani wala call him Rahul.

Santi   Rahuuuul.

Naz   Over there! In the lake.

Santi   In our lake?

They stare.

Naz   Hai Allah! Santi, kya karo gee? **(What are you going to do?)**

Santi What's he doing here?

Naz It's hot, yaar.

Santi So hot.

Naz Tujhe kya ho raha? (**What's happening to you?**)

Santi I'm fine.

Naz You look like you're going to explode.

Santi He swims so elegantly.

Naz Eh?

Santi Like a mermaid.

Naz Oh you got it bad.

Santi Got what?

Naz *It*. That thing nah. You know?

Santi How do *you* know?

Naz I just do.

Santi Tell me the word.

Naz Not everything has words, Santi, sometimes you just feel it.

Santi In my belly?

Naz Sometimes.

Santi Where do you feel it?

Naz For Rahul?

Santi Or anyone else? (*Beat.*) You can tell me . . .

Naz I feel it here.

Santi For?

Naz Why are you so scared of him?

Santi I'm not.

Naz   I'll tell you the word, when you talk to Rahul. Let's go.

Santi   No, Naz. No! I look –

Naz   You look fine. Chalo.

Santi   Not now, I don't want to. He's going to think we've been spying on him.

Naz   We have.

Santi   Not yet, Naz. Please.

Naz   Fine. But you're not getting your book back until you do.

Santi   Just means you'll have to read it.

Naz   Never! Kabhee bhee nahin.

She throws the book into the lake. **Santi** *doesn't know whether to go get it, or tell her off.*

Santi's Premonition

Santi   I had a dream. I had a dream you drowned in the lake and Lord Vishnu came and took you away to be his bride. You were blue and your eyes were closed and you were so still. Bilkul chup **(completely quiet)**.

I begged him to leave you, to take me. 'Take me,' I said.

He wouldn't listen so I jumped in. I dove in deep and kept swimming down, down. It was deeper than you could ever imagine. I swam for years and I still couldn't reach the bottom. Vishnu appeared in the water and conjured the reeds to capture me. Their leaves rose up and dragged me down.

Engulfing me into the darkness, I felt awash with sadness. I had lost you. We were both lost.

The Lihaf

Santi   Where did you get *this*?!

Naz   I found it.

Santi   You found a book?

Naz   I find things, I know how to get things. I got connections you know.

Santi   Naz! Seriously, where did you get it?

Naz   That's for me to know and for you to never find out.

Santi   Did you steal it?

Naz   Wow. You just jumped straight to stealing. I'll take it back if that's what you think –

Santi   No – wait, I – Thank you. I just want to know how you got it. Because you know it's –

Naz   Saima's brother gave it to me.

Santi   Since when do you know Saima's brother?

Naz   I know him.

Santi   A boy?

Naz   I know boys . . .

Santi *gives* **Naz** *a look.*

Naz   Fine, I know Saima, she took me to her brother's shop.

Santi   And he just gave it to you?

Naz   No . . . I told him that I wanted to get my friend a present and that it had to be extra special because. Well, because you're you. He said this one was perfect for girls like me –

Santi   He said that?

Naz   He said it was very popular and it would make the best present – Do you want to read it or nah?

Santi   Naz, you know what this is?

Naz   Hai Allah Santi, what? Is it a limited addition or something?

Santi   Edition.

Naz   That's what I meant. It's just a book, yaar.

Santi   No, it's not. It's THE book. The one everyone's talking about.

Naz   Are they?

Santi   It's been banned! Oh! I can't bear to touch it!

Naz   Give me –

Naz *goes to snatch it away,* **Santi** *tears it away.*

Santi   Mine!

Naz   I just want to see!

Santi   Let me smell it.

Naz   Weird. Santi you get weirder and weirder every day, you know. I don't know why I spend time with you.

Santi   You just don't appreciate good things.

Naz   I appreciate you.

Santi   Come. Sit, I'll read to you. You're going to lose your mind.

The girls settle in. **Santi** *makes a big deal of getting comfortable and assumes an air of grandeur. She begins as if she were an orator.*

Lihaaf by Ismat Chughtai. In winter when I put a quilt over myself, its shadows on the wall seem to sway like an elephant. That sets my mind racing into the labyrinth of times past. Memories come crowding in –

Naz   Boring!

Santi   Be patient nah, there's more.

Naz *snatches the book from* **Santi** *and skims it, she reaches a section and becomes wide-eyed.*

Naz   Ya Allah! What is this? (*She reads.*) I began rubbing her back which was smooth as the top of a table. I rubbed gently and was happy to be of some use to her. I don't understand.

Santi   She's making her maid rub her back. Her maid . . . is *rubbing* her back.

Naz (*she reads*)   'Here . . . a little below the shoulder . . . that's right . . . Ah! what pleasure . . . She expressed her satisfaction between sensuous breaths. How proud I felt!'

Santi   Your eyebrows are all wonky . . . what's wrong?

Naz   What are they doing? (*Continues reading.*) 'Come here and lie down beside me . . . She made me lie down with my head on her arm.' (*Beat.*) That's two women.

Santi   You know why it's so controversial, don't you?

Naz (*reading*)   'How skinny you are . . . your ribs are coming out. She began counting my ribs. I tried to protest.' She's touching her maid? And she, she –

Santi   You know what happened to the writer –

Naz   Why would you show me this?

Santi   You got it for *me*!

Naz   I can't believe you made me read it . . .

Santi   I didn't *make* you – Everyone knows why Lihaaf was banned!

Naz   I've never heard of it before. And now I know why, it's . . . This is . . . it's – I can't –

Santi *laughs at* **Naz** *getting worked up.*

Naz   What? What's so funny?

Santi   You! I can't believe Saima's brother gave you this, he must have been laughing –

Naz   Reading makes you ugly. Everyone knows that.

Santi   Just calm down . . .

Naz   No!

Santi   Naz . . .

Santi *waits for a response.* **Naz** *regrets her outburst but can't find the words to apologise.* **Santi** *leaves.* **Naz** *picks up the book again and hesitantly begins to read.*

Naz's Dream

Naz I rub her back. Let me count your ribs I say. She lets me. She wants me to. How proud I feel. Something is trying to escape. But I won't let it. Kabhee bhee nahin.

My hand turns into Rahul's and we hold our Santi close. She is magic, the way she moves in our arms.

The sun fills the sky and blinds me a little. I see her, in the middle of a waterfall. Naked, bathing, floating. And then suddenly other bodies, all naked and bathing and floating. Hundreds. Thousands. I turn to remove my own clothes to join them, but by the time I step into the milky water it has turned to red.

Nadeem the Tailor, Late 1945

The girls are in the village, a town car attracts their attention.

Santi   Woahh. Did your baba get a town car?

Naz   What? No! That can't be our car.

Santi   Why not? You have money.

Naz   Not *that* much money.

Santi   Who is that man?

Naz   Never seen him before.

Santi   Look at that moustache. It looks like a slug.

Naz   Slugtash!

Santi   Ewww – Why do you have to make everything disgusting?

Naz   You're the one who said slug.

Santi   You think food gets stuck in there when he eats?

Naz   I think the slug eats the food, like slurp, glug slurp.

Santi   He's coming closer.

Naz   Where's my dupatta **(scarf)**?

Santi *watches* **Naz** *fiddle with her clothing.*

Santi   What are you doing?

Naz   Hiding my shame.

Santi   No! He should lower his gaze.

They both stare in the direction of the man.

Naz   I can't tell if it's his slugtache that stinks of keema **(minced meat)** or his breath. He's totally going to be your husband. Keema breath and Santi sitting in a tree, K – I – S – S slurp slurp.

Santi   Ewww, not with that moustache! I bet he tickles his wife with it. Urgh.

Naz   You're just saying that because you prefer Rahul as a husband.

Santi   No –

Naz   Rahul and Santi sitting in a tree, K – I – S – S –

Santi   I think your baba knows keema breath.

Naz   No way!

Santi   He just gave him a massive hug!

Both   Ewwwwww.

Naz's father calls to her.

Naz   I don't want to go over there. My Ammi will shout if she sees me without my dupatta!

Naz's father calls again.

Naz   Aar rahee hoon. **(I'm coming.)**

Santi   That's 'cause you're getting boobs.

Naz   Been staring, have you?

Santi   He's getting angry.

Naz's father calls yet again.

Naz   Come with me?

Santi   You go. I'll find your dupatta.

Naz   Meet me later?

Santi   Only if you promise to tell me everything.

Naz   Of course!

The girls wink at each other.

Santi (*returning to 1949*)   I didn't know who that man was, but he was so arrogant. Watching him talk to your baba made my skin crawl. It was even worse when he turned his attention to you.

Naz (*still in the memory*)   Assalamualaikum, uncle.

Santi   His eyes looked like they wanted to eat you up. How dare he look at you like that? Couldn't he tell you didn't like it? You were clearly squirming. And it's like your baba was almost . . . He was encouraging it.

'Beta, this is Nadeem,' he said, so pleased with himself.

Naz   My mangetar (**betrothed**).

Santi   I didn't know if you understood what that word meant. What it really meant to be intended for someone. So I stood for a moment trying to hear what you were saying, but there was too much noise on the street. I tried to work out what was going on, but none of it made any sense to me.

Later, whilst you were engrossed in the trinkets Nadeem had brought with him from Rawalpindi I forced myself to swallow down a feeling of dread that ran deeper than forgetting that I'd promised you I'd go back to find your dupatta.

Election Season, January 1946

Soundscape of provincial election propaganda.

Naz   Nimboo Paani? **(Lemonade?)**

Santi   I'm not thirsty.

Naz   You don't want to see your boyfriend?

Santi   What?

Naz   I've seen you staring. Every time we go for nimboo paani you start to drool, and I know you don't love nimboo paani *that* much.

Santi   I – I don't drool.

Naz   You know, I would love some nimboo paani to quench my thirst. *Rahul, can you quench my thirst?*

Santi   You can't say that!

Naz   Does it make you all shy? Why are you so nervous?

Santi   You're gross.

Naz   Come on, you could go and do some voting with Rahul.

Santi   Voting?

Naz   Seriously, Santi, I didn't think anyone could be as boring as you, but then Rahul came along.

Santi   Do you even know what the elections are about?

Naz   Of course! It's a vote to see if India will become Muslim.

Santi   That's not it.

Naz   Yes it is. They keep telling people to vote for All India Muslim League.

Santi   That's not what that means.

Naz   Whatever, Santi. It's been months, Rahul's going to think you're deaf or mute or something.

Santi   These elections are important Naz, my baba said / this could really change our country.

Naz   / Just go talk to *him* about it. How else are you going to get him to talk to you?

When **Santi** *doesn't respond* **Naz** *launches into a song –*

Naz   Ayy baby!

Santi   Naz?

Naz   Ayy baby, Ayy Ji. Idhar ao! **(Come here!)**

Santi   Naz!

Naz   Idhar ao! **(Come here!)**

Santi   Fine, aa gaya. **(Here I am.)**

Naz   Behet jao. **(Sit down.)**

Santi   Behet gaya. **(I've sat down.)**

Naz   Uth Jao. **(Get up.)**

Santi   Uth gaya. **(I'm up.)**

Naz   Ghoom jao. **(Turn around.)**

Santi   Ghoom gaya. **(I've turned around.)**

Naz   Ab bolo kya khaogay? **(Now tell me, what will you eat?)**

Santi   Jalebi. **(Sweet snack.)**

Naz   No! You say nimboo paani! OOff! OK, again. Ayy baby . . .?

Santi (*more into it now*)   Ayy ji.

Naz   Ay baby!

Santi   Ayy ji.

Naz   Idhar ao!

Santi   Aa gaya.

Santi twirls into Naz's arms and there's a moment between them. Naz leans in and kisses Santi on the cheek. They giggle.

Naz   Behet jao.

Santi   Behet gaya.

Naz   Uth jao.

Santi   Uth gaya.

Naz   Ghoom jao.

Santi   Ghoom gaya.

Naz   Ab bolo kya khaogay?

Santi   Nimbo paani!

Naz twirls Santi around and into her arms again. She goes to kiss Santi, but this time Santi kissers her.

Both   Ayy baby.

Santi   I love you, Naz, you make everything better.

Naz looks to Santi as if to kiss her. When she doesn't go for it, Naz brushes it off.

Naz   Chalo, speak to me as if I'm Rahul.

Santi   I CAN'T. I CAN'T.

Naz   Just talk to me. Him.

Naz puffs out her chest and pretends to be Rahul.

Santi   You're too silly.

Naz (*as* **Rahul**)   Who you calling silly, girl? I am a fine specimen of a man. Just look at me.

As Rahul she flexes her muscles and kisses her biceps.

Naz (*as* **Rahul**)   Oh, you like that, do you? Silly girl. If you like that then you should see what I've got under my dhoti (**traditional male garment**)!

She grabs at where her crotch would be and runs after **Santi**.

(*As* **Rahul**.) What are you running for? Hey girl . . . Come back here. I've got something for you.

They chase each other.

Naz (*as* **Rahul**)   Yo. Chill out, it's just pamphlets. I heard you're into reading.

Santi   What?

Naz (*as herself*)   Tell him about all the books you've read.

Santi   He doesn't care about that.

Naz   He will.

Santi   I could just flick my hair like you do . . .

Naz   Chal, let me see.

Santi *does super awkwardly.*

Naz   Oh no. Here. Like this.

Naz *demonstrates. It's very seductive.* **Santi** *repeats rigidly.*

Naz   Bus (**stop**).

Santi   No! Again!

Naz   You're more than just your hair, Santi, why can't you see that?

Santi   You're not helping though.

Naz   Fine, fine. I'll be serious. Just how you like it. Serious and boring –

Santi   Yes, OK, thank you.

Naz *becomes* **Rahul**. *She sets up the parameters of the nimboo paani stall and then seeing* **Santi**, *immediately thrusts a pamphlet at her.* **Santi** *takes a moment to read it.*

Santi   Oh, Hindustan for Hindus?

Naz (*as* **Rahul**)   Yes. We are taking back our country one village at a time.

Santi   Taking it back from who?

Naz (*as* **Rahul**)   Wote Congress in the next election.

Santi   Did you write this?

Naz (*as* **Rahul**)   Nehruji will take care of everything.

Santi   Where is India going? Who are they taking it back from –

Naz (*as* **Rahul**)   British of course.

Santi   Ohhhhhhhhh. Your ideas are very . . . sophisticated.

Naz (*as* **Rahul**)   What is this word . . . so . . . soph . . . sophistic? Very big word. You must have very big brain.

Santi   I do.

Naz (*as* **Rahul**)   I have very big . . .

The two begin to walk towards each other.

Santi   Yes . . .?

Naz (*as* **Rahul**)   Arms.

Santi   And eyes.

Naz (*as* **Rahul**)   You have noticed?

Santi   I have.

Naz (*as* **Rahul**)   What else have you noticed?

Santi   Your hair, it's . . . very glossy.

Naz, *without realising flicks it.*

Naz (*as* **Rahul**)   Isn't it?

Santi   Yes.

Naz   I like your eyes too.

Santi   I think I've got a squint, too many books.

Naz   Suits you.

Naz, *somewhere between herself and* **Rahul** *brushes a hair off* **Santi**'s *face.* **Santi** *giggles.*

Santi   Log kya kaehengay? **(What will people say?)**

Naz (*no longer as* **Rahul**)   I don't care what people say.

Naz *kisses her on the lips this time. Unsure what to do* **Santi** *draws away. A movement sequence leads into* **Naz**'s *dream and continues throughout.*

Naz   There is a waterfall. Cascading words and memories illuminated by the streaks of evening light in the air.

I climb into the water and let Santi wash my hair with the juice of a mango. It feels like she is washing away my sins. With each stroke I am made new again. I am at peace.

Santi Meets Rahul on the Road

Santi   I was walking from the gurdwara to your house and – there he was. Tall and handsome, and walking straight towards me. I feel the heat on my face. My cheeks flush. My feet start to drag, I slow down, just so I'll have longer to stare. And then –

He looks back! At me! He is looking straight at me. I can't look away. Eyes away, Santi! Eyes away. You can look anywhere but at his face! His face is glowing, smiling. Smiling at me. At me? He's smiling at me? No way. No way no way.

He grabs my hand and pulls me close. He tells me that Jinnah is a fool, and Sikhs and Hindus have to stick together now.

I breathe him in. His scent enters me and it is like steam working its way into my mind. His hand is not soft. It is just the right kind of rough and I imagine it tracing circles on my skin. I shudder in a way that I have never before. The electricity between us makes the hair on my arms stand on end. I want to dive into the lake and feel the vibrations of the ripples he makes deep inside of me.

Naz *awakes from a bad dream directly into 1946 where a soundscape of a speech by Jinnah takes us into the next scene.*

Jinnah   One India is impossible to realise. It will inevitably mean that the Muslim will be transferred from the domination of the British to the caste Hindu rule. A position that Muslim will never accept.

17th August, 1946 (Day after Day of Direct Action and Calcutta Killings)

Naz   Santi, Santi, guess what I just witnessed? / Is witnessed the right word?

Santi   / What? What did you see?

Naz   Ammi asked me to go and get some saffron, right?

Santi   What's the special occasion?

Naz   Nadeem's sister is coming – She got married and went to England.

Santi   Oh.

Naz   Ammi wants me to bring saffron for the biryani.

Santi   Fancy.

Naz   I had the saffron in my hand and was coming back by the lake. At first I saw lots of people crowding. I thought maybe someone had fallen in – and then I saw loads of blood in the mud. It was a mutilated donkey.

Santi   Donkey?

Naz   There was so much blood and flesh that had become part of the mud so much that we couldn't tell where the donkey stopped and the mud began.

Santi   Ew.

Naz   And the head – it was hanging like urgh, you know how on Eid we see goats being halal-ed . . .?

She makes the gesture for a goat having its throat slit with blood spurting everywhere.

Well, it was nothing like that.

Santi   Why are you telling me this?

Naz   I asked Abba if people were still doing sacrifice for Eid and he said that it was a donkey and not a goat. And then he called me a ghadhi **(female donkey)**.

Santi You *are* a gadhi **(an ass)**.

Naz I couldn't stop looking at the head and the blood and then when Abba tried to move the body, the head didn't move. The threads that kept it together almost snapped like when you pull the elastic on your pyjama too much.

Santi Bus nah. Too much.

Naz I just kept smelling the saffron to make sure I wasn't going to be sick. Something's going on. Abba said it was a threat from the Hindus.

Santi Why?

Naz I don't know! They didn't even sharpen the knife properly, you could tell from the bone that it was so jagged.

Santi How do you know so much about slaughtering animals?

Naz Everyone knows you have to sharpen the knife to give it a clean cut. Everyone except Hindus.

Santi Why are the Hindus threatening us?

Naz I don't know.

Santi Didn't you ask?

Naz I was too busy checking out the donkey.

Santi Can you ask, please.

Naz We'll be OK, right? It's only donkeys –

Santi Ask your Abba. He always knows what's going on . . .

Naz Only if you come with me to get some more saffron? I dropped what I bought in the blood.

Santi Deal.

Rain. They both return to 1949.

Diwali, October 1946

Santi   I got you something.

Naz   What?

Santi   Close your eyes.

Naz   Santi, just –

Santi   Close your eyes, Naz!

Naz (*she does*)   You know my Simran thinks it's weird we give Diwali gifts to each other.

Santi   Simran's weird.

Naz   What's taking so long?

Santi *unfolds a dupatta.* **Naz** *opens her eyes.*

Santi   I made it. Well my Ammi helped me make it. See there in the corner, a little S and N. In English, of course. To remind you to study –

Naz   Santi, it's beautiful.

Santi   Now you can keep me with you everywhere. You better not lose it.

Naz   Kabhee bhee nahin. My turn.

Santi   Wait. Let me close my eyes.

She does and immediately –

Naz   Open them!

Naz *hands* **Santi** *a gold bangle.*

Santi   WOW. What is this?

Naz   A kangan (**bangle**)! For someone that reads so much you're such a duffer sometimes you know.

Santi   Naz, this . . . it's gold.

Naz   Yeah, I think so.

Santi   How did you? Where did you?

Naz   Don't you worry about that.

Santi   Naz, I know your Ammi would not have given you the money, for this, not, not for me –

Naz   What do you mean not for you? You're my Santi, aren't you? I want to see how it sparkles on your wrist.

Santi *puts it on.*

Naz   Hai Santi, mashallah, you look so beautiful.

Santi   Did Nadeem give you this?

Naz   What does it matter?

Santi   I don't want it!

Naz   What?

Santi   I don't want it. If Nadeem gave it to you I don't want it on my wrist.

Naz   No. It is a gift for you.

Santi   A gift that was given to you.

Naz   He's not so bad you know, Santi. He has a nice moustache.

Santi   Well great.

Naz   Baba says he makes a lot of money in Pindi –

Santi   Rawalpindi?

Naz   He bought me all sorts of things. Silks and gold and –

Santi   This gold kangan?

Naz   You should see the suits! And he brought luddoo (**a special sweet**). I'll share everything with you. He has a Jinnah hat. I'm going to steal it and then we can play –

Santi   You can't steal his hat.

Naz   Can too. He says I'm his little chiriya **(bird)** and I can have anything I want. I'm going to work for him – model clothes for him and make chai, and we'll live a good life.

Santi   In Rawalpindi?

Naz   Maybe. Baba says I'll be safer over there.

Santi   Why are you unsafe here?

Naz   Change is coming.

Santi   Change is good.

Naz   Anyway, you're going to be coming with me!

Santi   What?

Naz   Of course!

Santi   What will I do?

Naz   Work with me, for Nadeem.

Santi   Naz –

Naz   You think I'd go anywhere without you?

Santi   I don't think that's what your baba is suggesting – You said he was your mangetar **(betrothed)** –

Naz   So? You can still come.

Santi   I don't think you understand.

Naz   What have you got here?

Santi   Who will feed the goats?

Naz   The goats will learn to live without you.

Santi   You'll learn to live without me!

A grand gesture from **Naz**.

Naz   Never. Kabhee bee nahin. **(Never.)** For as long as there is barsaat, you will be my friend.

It starts to rain.

Santi (*returning to 1949*)   For as long as there is barsaat, you will be my friend.

The rain fades.

Skimming Stones

Naz *is sitting by the tree at the lake, trying to study. She is learning catchphrases by rote.* **Santi** *is skimming stones.*

Naz   Too many cooks ruin the . . . too many cooks ruin the broth. Should be saalan **(curry)**. Or biryani. No one knows what broth is.

Santi   NAZ! Ao nah **(come on)**, teach me.

Naz   I'm studying. Too many cooks ruin the broth. Too many cooks ruin the broth.

Santi   Spoil.

Naz   You know this stuff doesn't come naturally to me.

Santi   What are you even learning?

Naz   Proverbs.

Santi   Hai, proverbs, look at you.

Naz   Absence makes the heart grow fonder.

Santi   Kya?

Naz   Absence makes the heart grow fonder. What's fonder?

Santi   Fonder means affectionate, like love.

Naz   Oh.

They sit for a moment. **Naz** *reading,* **Santi** *writing.*

Santi   Naz, yeh suno. **(Listen to this.)**

Naz   Do I have to?

Santi   Please. I wrote something I want to share with you.

Naz   You want to share your shayari **(poetry)** with me? Your heart touching poetry?

Santi   Heartfelt.

Naz   Oh, your heart is feeling me, not touching me.

Santi   Promise you won't laugh.

Naz   I promise.

Santi   I see you.

Naz   Wah!

Santi   That's just the title.

Naz   I knew that.

Santi

> I see you, in the shadows
> that the leaves of the trees make, in the
> way the sun sets
> over our village, in water that
> gives home to the fish.

Naz   It's fishes.

Santi *glares*.

Naz   OK, sorry, go on.

Santi

> I see you in my own reflections
> in mirrors.
> I want to break the mirrors
> and bleed but even then
> I think I would see
> only you
> in my blood.
> I do not see
> with my eyes anymore.
> I only see
> with my heart
> and even my heart beats
> your name at every step.
> Do you see me too?
> Does your heart
> beat San-ti,
> San-ti, San-ti,

like mine beats for yours?
I want to love you more
than even you
love yourself.
I see you.
Do you see me?

Naz   Yes.

Santi   Yes?

Naz   Yes, I see you.

Santi   It's a rhetorical question, Naz.

Naz   What's rhetorical?

Santi   It means you don't need to answer it. What did you think? Of my poem?

Naz   It doesn't rhyme.

Santi   This is modern poetry, Naz, modern poetry doesn't always rhyme. It has rhythm. Like a heartbeat.

Naz   I liked the Sa-an-ti bit.

Santi   It's San-ti. Two beats, San-ti.

Naz *tries and beats her chest as she beats* **Santi***'s name.*

Naz   Sa-an-ti.

Naz *tries and beats her chest as she says* **Santi***'s name.*

Santi   San-ti, San-ti, San-ti.

Naz   Who did you write this about?

Santi   No one.

Naz   Is it about me?

Santi   Naz, you know I love you, right?

Naz   I know.

Santi *tries to extricate herself from* **Naz**'s *arms, but* **Naz** *is holding on tightly. It's cute for a moment but then* **Santi** *struggles, she wants out. They jostle.* **Naz** *grips tighter, and then suddenly lets go. The energy of their scuffle takes us into –*

The Indian Problem, March 1947

A soundscape of a Pathé newsreel plays announcing the arrival of Jinnah in London to meet with the Viceroy of India to discuss the transfer of power post-Partition.

As it finishes, we find **Santi** *trying to explain to* **Naz** *the appointment of Mountbatten as Viceroy of India. Although it looks like the game they're used to playing, it doesn't feel fun anymore.*

Santi (*as Clement Attlee*)   His Majesty has been pleased to approve, as successor to Lord Wavell, the appointment of Mountbatten as Viscount of India, who will be entrusted with the task of transferring to Indian hands the responsibility for the government of British India in the manner that will best ensure the future happiness and prosperity of India.

Naz (*as herself*)   What about Pakistan?

Santi   I didn't hear them say anything about that.

Naz (*as herself*)   But why *now*?

Santi   Nuh uh. You have to . . .

She gestures that **Naz** *should be rounder like Churchill.* **Naz** *doesn't want to.*

Naz   What's going to happen next?

Santi *glares at* **Naz**. *Gestures again, even bigger this time.*

Santi   Fine.

Naz *assumes the role of Churchill with a cigar in one hand and whisky glass in the other.*

Naz (*as Churchill*)   You don't just wake up and think, 'Oh, let us get another viscount'. What are you not telling us?

Santi *nods, satisfied and then proceeds.*

Santi (*as Clement Attlee*)   Oh well well well you know . . . The last viscount was soooo awful at his job, we had to get rid of him. It was thought that in the changing phase of the Indian problem, it was a suitable time to make a change.

Naz (*as herself*)   Eh? We're not a problem.

Santi (*as Clement Attlee*)   Aren't you?

Naz (*as herself*)   Why do they think we're a problem?

Santi (*as herself*)   Come on, there's lots more . . . Churchill has this great bit where everyone is asking him questions at the same time and he, he just can't –

Naz   I don't want to play.

Santi   What else are we going to do? Sit around and wait?

Naz   It feels like it's getting closer and closer and –

Santi   Do you really think whatever is going on will affect our little village?

Naz   Don't *you*?

Santi   It doesn't have to.

Naz   I think it already has.

Santi *fades away as* **Naz** *enters the dreamscape.*

Naz   I play Mountbatten, playing viceroy. Ruler of a country he's never even been to before arriving last month.

(*As Mountbatten.*) I draw a line. A line, a line, a liiiiiine.

(*As herself.*) I wait for Santi to return. To order me to speak in English.

(*As Mountbatten.*) I draw a line through her heart. Split her in two, or three. Or more? Which side will you be on? Which side will she?

(*As herself.*) It doesn't matter if you're Sikh or I'm Muslim, we'll all get big, beautiful bungalas of our own. And when it rains we'll dance on the verandah.

(*As Mountbatten.*) But only when I finish carving up hearts with crayons.

(*As herself.*) I know I am not him, but I feel him in me. I hold his ultimate power in my hands. My mouth speaks San-ti, San-ti, San-ti. With every new utterance a soldier appears, but still, I can not stop saying her name . . . until I have spoken an entire army of Angrez.

They march through Rahul's lake and then I see her. Santi stands on the bed of the river. She stands between the rifts of the earth and it is like she is standing on the other side of the world of me.

Teeyan, July 1947

Santi *is preparing for Teeyan.* **Naz** *arrives.*

Santi   Hain? Yeh, kya? **(Hey, what's this?)** Why aren't you ready?

Naz   Abba said I can't go.

Santi   Why?

Naz   I have to get ready to go.

Santi   Now?

Naz   Soon. Before . . . before it –

Santi   Before what?

Naz   Nothing.

Santi   Naz! If you know something, you have to tell me.

Naz *doesn't want to, but –*

Naz   Rahul's goondas **(thugs)** are dangerous.

Santi   Rahul doesn't have thugs. He – He's about words, he's like Gandhi. He doesn't believe in violence.

Naz   I heard him. I heard Rahul talking about a train to a man in a bloody shirt. A train of dead people.

Santi   Maybe Rahul went to help them?

Naz   They were all dead, all of them. Hundreds of them. All dirty Muslims, he said. All dead, all headed east.

Santi   Where east? We don't even know what's going to happen yet.

Naz   But there *will* be a Pakistan, Santi. Jinnah said it himself.

Santi   Who cares what Jinnah says, he's a joke.

Naz   Don't say that. Qaid-e-Azam wants a place for us, somewhere we can belong.

Santi   You belong with me, Naz. Here, in our village, or have your dreams gotten too big? Jinnah doesn't care about Muslims. He said so himself.

Naz   Wherever Pakistan will be, Muslims will move there. Just like those people on the train wanted to move, but they never got to where they wanted to go, and now I can't go to Teeyan even though I want to and Santi I think I understand the donkey now.

Santi   Ghadhi, calm down. You don't even know if this train of dead people actually exists or whatever –

Naz   Are you so blinded by Rahul that you can't see what's going on? / I thought you were the clever one.

Santi   / Who are you to lecture me? You can't see what's right in front of your face.

Naz   Your fazool **(stupid)** face is in front of my face, and right now I don't like it.

Santi   Run along then. To your precious baba and Nadeem and see where that leads you. You of all people should know better than to put your faith in these stupid men.

Naz   It's not the same anymore, Santi, why can't you see that?

Santi   I know. But it's Teeyan, if you don't come tonight what will happen tomorrow?

Naz   We can still be together – We had a plan, remember?

Santi   Naz! Pakistan is not for me –

Naz   You *have* to come.

Santi   And do what? Cook for you? Clean for you? Rub your back? Wait on you like you were some memsaab **(Madam)**?

Naz   Santi –

Santi   Grow up, Naz. You know that's what's coming. What he expects. Think about his teeth, all yellow from tobacco. Think about kissing that.

Naz   It's not that bad!

Santi   He shouldn't be kissing you.

Naz   Who knew you were such a prude! I can kiss you but not Nadeem? Is that how it is?

Santi   You cannot marry him, Naz. You won't be safe. You'll always have to hide who you are and what if he – I'm scared what might happen to you, what he might –

Naz   You're just jealous.

Santi   Jealous?

Naz   You think Rahul's going to want a boring face like you? He's got an education, he could have any city girl he wants. He doesn't want you. No one wants you.

Santi   Is that what you really think?

Naz   Even *I* don't want you.

Santi   At least I like Rahul, at least I know *how* to like Rahul.

Naz   What's that mean?

Santi   You know.

Naz   What?

Santi   You're not going to be able to do it.

Naz   What?

Santi   Your wedding night.

Naz   What about it?

Santi   You know what happens?

Naz   Of course.

Santi   You know Maryam?

Naz   What about her?

Santi   Everyone said that it was her fault, what happened to her. Because she couldn't – When she got married, she didn't do it – And that's why she's dead, Naz.

Naz   . . .

Santi   Everyone knows Muslim men beat their wives.

Naz   Santi! Why would you say that? / That's not what you really think, is it?

Santi   / Beat them to death.

Naz   . . .

Santi   She refused and look what happened.

Naz   . . .

Santi   Bolo! **(Speak!)**

Naz   . . .

Santi   Thought so.

Naz's Dream, 1949

Naz I dream of Santi melting into the water. I jump in to join her but she's not there. I force myself down to find her. The reeds begin to bubble and fizz and hiss to the surface, destroying everything between us. I can not let this pass.

So I dive deeper and deeper. Something is drawing me down and I cannot stop. Not now, not ever. As the water fills my lungs, my lips turn blue. I try to lick them back to life.

Now I wear the flag of Pak-e-istan like a shroud, almost proudly. Forgetting that the weight of it forces all the air out of my lungs. Somedays I catch the smell of nimboo paani and I remember who I am and where I came from.

Partition Draws Closer, August 1947

Santi   Walking home from the Gurdwara feels different now. I focus on my feet. Watch them throw dust into the air. I will the clouds of dirt to envelop me, protect me from passers by.

Something compels me to look up and there he is! Walking straight towards me. I feel the familiar sensation rising. I allow myself a moment to admire his hair and it's like there is a fire in my chest. Warmth rises from my stomach to my face and –

Eyes away, Santi! Eyes away. You can look anywhere but at his face! It takes all of my strength, but I do. As I turn my head, I catch his smile, it dazzles me. I watch as he raises his perfect arm to the sky to wave. I follow the line of his gaze to a group of men in the distance, all raising their own hands in response. With friendly waves and . . . wielding swords? Swords and machetes! Sharp, piercing instruments covered in blood. I blink through the sunlight, it must be a mirage?

It's not real, Santi! It *can't* be real! His sing-song laughter fills my ears. Its beautiful melody reassures me that whatever is coming, Rahul will fight for us. He will stand up to them, his intelligent rhetoric will keep the violence at bay.

But then I see the glint of the sun reflect off the dagger hanging out of his pocket and I realise that he's running towards them. His smile, his laughter is *in support* of them.

I realise he's one of them . . . They are his people . . . and I no longer know who are mine.

Engagement Party, 1947

Santi (*from 1949*)   When I heard your baba was throwing a party I was worried it might attract the wrong kind of attention. I had to check. But when I got there I couldn't face you. I hated what I'd said to you. I couldn't bear the thought that they might be the last words you'd ever hear from my mouth.

Naz   I told you not to come.

Santi   Who died and made you the general?

Naz   My party. Apparently.

Santi   Ah yes, Naz Bibi is getting married, we must obey her. Do you hear that everyone? Naz, queen of all who are betrothed has ordered me, her saheli to leave.

I'm going anyway. Enjoy your party and keema breath. Make sure he trims his moustache before the big night, don't want you to –

Naz   You look beautiful.

Santi   *You* look beautiful.

Naz   He's made it himself. The gold gota **(lace trim)** and the silk is so soft and expensive. Ammi ordered all of these fresh flowers for me and I'm going to have them in my hair and the bedroom for . . .

Santi   You were right about Rahul. I'm sorry I didn't see it before. I'm sorry I didn't realise how dangerous his words were. He doesn't have goondas, he is a goonda / and Naz, I don't know what to do but –

Naz   / Santi, I don't want to.

Santi   So don't.

Naz   Nadeem wants to leave as soon as possible. Just in case.

Santi   So we take back control.

Naz   How? He won't leave me alone. Everywhere I look he's there. Gifts, and mithai **(confectionery)** and that ugly slugface.

Santi   Tell your baba you don't want to do this.

Naz   Abba says it's happening no matter what. It's best –

Santi   What does your mama say?

Naz   Everyone listens to Abba. No one cares about me!

Santi   I care about you.

Naz   I can't stand him. Not even the suits and presents can make up for it. He's horrible. He shouts at me and calls me churail **(witch)**. He calls me a witch and he – He – He doesn't like me. I'm scared that he really doesn't like me.

A voice calls for **Naz**.

Naz   Santi, you have to help.

Santi   You could just donk him? With a vhelan **(rolling pin)**?

Naz   Santi! This is serious.

Santi   OK . . . You should be the worst wife ever!

Naz   And?

Santi   Burn the chai!

Naz   Burn the rotis so he never has anything to eat.

Santi   Drop the plates.

Naz   I could get ugly.

Santi   You could not give him kids!

Naz   That really is the worst wife ever.

A voice calls again for **Naz**.

Naz   What can I do *today*? Right now? To make him leave . . . without me?

Santi   You could be so much trouble that he doesn't want anything to do with you.

Naz   We could push him into the lake!

Santi   With all his clothes on!

Naz   Steal his clothes and then run away –

Santi   He'd have to run all the way home naked.

Both   Taubah taubah taubah. **(Shame shame shame.)**

Santi   Ew, but then we'd have to see him naked!

Naz   Taubah taubah taubah.

Santi   Can you imagine what everyone would say?

Both   Taubah taubah taubah.

Santi   You'd have to give all the engagement presents back.

Naz   But he'll be so angry he'll never want to look at me again.

Santi   He'll go away.

Naz   And I won't have to marry him.

Santi   He's so gross everyone will be happy they can forget about him.

Naz   Everyone will forget keema breath and his silly moustache.

Santi   So we'll take him to the lake . . .?

Naz   We'll take him to the lake.

They shake on it.

A Deal with Destiny, August 1947

A soundscape repeats Nehru's speech about independence.

Nehru   Long years ago, we made a tryst with destiny, and now the time comes when we shall redeem our pledge, not wholly or in full measure, but very substantially. At the stroke of the midnight hour, when the world sleeps, India will awake to life and freedom.

A moment comes, which comes but rarely in history, when we step out from the old to the new – when an age ends, and when the soul of a nation, long suppressed, finds utterance.

Santi *walks, swinging a cricket bat.*

Santi   My younger brother had been teaching me how to play cricket. I totally knew how to play cricket. I bowled better than all of them, but there was a whole afternoon to waste so I kept asking questions they couldn't answer. Then, when it was time I walked slowly over to the lake.

It's too hot, too humid. I want to dip my feet in water and lie underneath our tree, be cool before we . . . As I approach the bhor **(banyan tree)** I hear –

Naz *(V/O)*   One, two, three, four, five . . .

(Spoken.) Just over here!

Santi   That's Naz! I'd recognise her voice anywhere.

Naz   I want to show you my favourite spot.

Santi   Naz and Nadeem are skimming stones into the lake. He laughs cruelly when her pebble plops into the water causing ripples. Even from here I can see how yellow his teeth are.

Naz *(V/O)*   Six, seven, eight, nine, ten steps to the left, three to the right . . . Perfect position to –

(Spoken.) Have you ever seen something so perfect?

Santi *(as Nadeem)*   Never, until now.

(*As herself.*) He takes a step towards her.

Naz (*V/O*)   Ugh, why are his eyes fixed on my chest?

His hand reaches out. She flinches.

(*Spoken.*) Come see how cool it is just over here.

Santi   She jumps under the shade of our tree. What's she playing at? I can't see her anymore.

Naz   The bhor keeps it shady all day long. Mmm. So nice. Isn't it?

Santi   He grabs her and pulls her close.

She squeezes her eyes shut and tries to wriggle out of his hold.

Santi   'Look at me,' he says. 'Look at me, look . . .'

Naz *opens her eyes to see* **Nadeem**.

Santi   He mutters something under his breath. I hear the sound of his palm hitting skin.

Naz *holds her face where* **Nadeem** *has slapped her.*

Naz   I won't obey you. I'll never obey you.

Santi   Naz is crying.

Naz   Let go of me. I hate you. I hate everyone.

Santi   HOW DARE YOU! HOW DARE YOU! HOW DARE YOU! I run straight at him. We're falling. He pulls me into the water. I can't – Nadeem's hands tighten around my throat. Water fills me. Water –

Naz   Santi is screaming under the surface. Her eyes are bulging. He's drowning her.

Santi   I can't breathe.

Naz   I pick up the bat. All I know is, I have to save her. I'll save you!

Santi   There is a growing pool of red in the water. Nadeem is face down and Naz stares at me with my brother's bat in her hand.

Naz   Jaldi! **(Quickly!)**

Santi   Run.

Naz   I'm not going to leave you.

Santi   I'm going too, in the other direction. I'll meet you by your house.

Naz   Nadeem is a Muslim man, Santi, who knows what will happen if you get caught!

Santi   It would be worse for you. Go now.

Naz *turns away and runs.* **Santi** *watches her.*

Santi   I watch her run away from me almost until she reaches the village. I watch her hair swing from side to side like an elephant's trunk until I am sure she won't turn back.

It begins to rain.

By the time Nadeem's body was discovered, everything had changed. The line had been drawn and our little village was officially a part of India. Naz's family were nowhere to be found. I prayed this meant they made it out alive. I prayed Pakistan was worth it.

When the lake flooded and our secret rose to the surface, baba told me that I owed my life to our community. That I would be forced to remember how lucky I am, lucky to be Indian.

1949

Santi   Outside the window the children buy nimboo paani on their way home from school. I can hear their excited chatter. It has been a hot day and they are thirsty. I don't need to look out of the window to know this. There is not much I need anymore. I have more notebooks than I could ever have longed for.

As I write, I wonder if there is a way to share my good luck with you. I try to recall your face but . . . I close my eyes and think of barsaat instead.

Both   It takes some time, but I begin to feel it. I feel it on my arms. I feel it in my hair.

Naz   I feel it in my belly.

Santi   I feel it in my ruha.

Both   Do you feel it too?

Naz   I think of you often at the foot of our tree, with your feet in the water as the rain splashes down. I hope you are free now friend.

Santi *finishes her book. She closes it and gently places it on the floor.*

Santi   Tum jiyo hazaron saal. **(May you live a thousand years)**.

Santi *exits.*

Naz   May you live a thousand years.

End of play.